THE **CANNABIS** **CONVERSATION**

Navigating the friction between fact, myth and Scripture

JAMES GOBEN

To my wife Darlene, who believes in me and pushes me to be my best. Your support, advice and even correction shape my writing into what it is today. I am forever grateful.

CONTENTS

INTRODUCTION

The worst distance between two people is misunderstanding.
NEETESH DIXIT

Without a doubt, cannabis is a controversial topic in the church world. Everyone you ask will likely have an opinion on the subject of cannabis. That in itself is not a problem. God has given each one of us a distinct personality along with freedom of opinion and belief. The Holy Spirit often guides us to individual convictions on things that Scripture does not specifically condone or condemn. The issue comes when we fail, either intentionally or unintentionally, to express those opinions in a way that is grace filled, or we refuse to listen and really hear those who believe differently than we do.

The church has not been good when it comes to having an open and honest discussion on topics that go against the status quo. Cannabis is certainly one of those topics where a civil dialog based on facts, not opinions, is hard to find. In many churches the conversation is shut down as quickly as it begins—if someone is even brave enough to approach the topic. In other churches the conversation quickly turns to the sin of one party (typically the pro-cannabis person) for the convictions they hold on this volatile subject.

The hardened views of yesteryear are beginning to fade, but there is still work to do. We, as Christians, owe it to our Savior to be open to having a civil discussion with those who do not think or believe as we do. This is the most fundamental part of evangelism in our post-modern culture.

We know those who are running from Jesus are looking for any and every excuse to justify their denial of Him. They will often go out of their way to find a reason to point fingers at the church. Unfortunately, we are often our own worst enemies and give the lost plenty of fuel for the fire in their rebellion against God. When the conversation breaks down because we are unprepared, or unwilling, to discuss a topic, the Kingdom suffers.

Luke gives us a great account of Paul's time in Athens in Acts chapter 17. As Paul wandered around the city, he saw things around him that were troubling, things that went against his beliefs. Instead of smashing idols and tearing down the people of Athens, he sought to use what they knew and believed as a bridge to introduce them to Jesus. That should be our goal when the discussion of cannabis, or any other controversial topic comes up. Regardless of which side of the debate you land on, we should seek to understand the other perspective so we can introduce the lost to Christ, not push them further away.

For you as a reader, the topic of cannabis may not be something you encounter often. For me, it is always present. God has called me to Colorado to reach the special needs/disabled community. When you live, work, and play here, the topic is always in your face. This state is full of medical refugees who left everything they knew for a chance to save their child's life. As a result, cannabis is serious medicine in this community of people. It is also a community where many are angry at God and wary of the church. Many in the special needs community have been hurt by church and/or Christian organizations.

Even in a state where recreational marijuana is legal, and has been for years, families are being thrown out of the church for their choice to use cannabis to stop their children's seizures. The people who need Jesus the most are, at times, being pushed away. I tend to believe that a vast majority of these cases are never meant to be malicious on either side. Instead, it is a breakdown in communication. This discussion has the potential to be emotionally charged, and trust me, families who have seen seizures reduced or stopped by cannabis will fight the hardest for what they know to be true. If we are not prepared to hear and acknowledge their view, things quickly go awry.

My goal for this book is not to convince you the reader that what you believe, and are convicted of, about cannabis is right or wrong. My goal is to present both sides of the discussion in a way that every reader closes the book more informed about the position and conviction of those on the other side of this sensitive topic. Hopefully, you will walk away with some additional understanding of your personal convictions too. I hope that I can present the facts and the arguments of each side in a way that promotes open and honest conversation— the kind that leads people to Jesus Christ.

My desire is to see believers on both sides of the debate equipped with the facts and truth about cannabis, specifically medical marijuana. When the facts are known, the discussion can move from defending

our specific position to hearing the other's side. It also opens the door
to being able to follow Paul's example in Acts 17 and use other people's beliefs to lead them to Christ.

A much as I've tried while writing this to remain unbiased, I am not
sure if I managed to do so. My opinion on this topic is, however, irrel-
evant. Each and every Christian has the duty to prayerfully consider
the facts and let the Holy Spirit lead us to a decision. My opinion is
not that of the Lord; it is only what the Spirit has convicted me of.
Yours may be different, but as long as it is a true conviction of the
Holy Spirit that has been prayed through, I will not consider it wrong.

I am a strong believer that our opinions pose some of the biggest
issues we have when discussions like this come up. Our opinions
are just that, opinions. An argument based on an opinion that may
be wrong turns defensive very quickly. When we have a discussion
that flows out of conviction, there is no reason to be defensive, or
at least there should not be. If we truly understand that each person
may have a different conviction or perspective on the gray areas of
Scripture or topics where the Bible is silent, then we can have a discussion in which both sides learn without simply trying to be right
or justifying their existing conviction.

My prayer is that this book will be a path to civil conversations about
cannabis that promotes healing and unity, not division. Knowledge
is the power that erases ignorance and promotes life-changing discussion. The more we know, the better Christians we are, and the
more effective we are for the Kingdom.

It is human nature to fear what we do not understand, even in the
church world. Satan loves fear and will use it every chance he can to

destroy the church. The more we know, the stronger we are. Stand firm in what you are convicted of, but in a way which does not give Satan room to destroy your witness.

May the Lord guide you through these sensitive discussions.

1

THE GROWING TREND

Why is marijuana against the law? It grows naturally
upon our planet. Doesn't the idea of making nature
against the law seem to you a bit ... unnatural?

BILL HICKS

We need grown-ups in charge in Washington to say marijuana
is not the kind of thing that ought to be legalized, it ought
not to be minimized, that it's in fact a very real danger.

JEFF SESSIONS

Marijuana. Pot. Weed. Medicine. No matter what you choose to call it, the cannabis plant is pushing its way into mainstream American culture. From movie references to prime-time news stories, the debate over marijuana has moved from seedy back alleys to the American living room. The shift in how Americans view marijuana creates new opportunities for discussion along with a new set of problems to be worked through, especially for the church.

The mere mention of marijuana likely stirs some emotion in you. For some, the long-held belief that cannabis is a gateway drug comes to mind. Others may flash back to a time in their past where smoking marijuana was a common event. Perhaps your mind jumps to a Cheech and Chong movie where cannabis is more comedy than something good or bad. For others, the mere mention of marijuana brings to mind all kinds of sin and debauchery the church must shun at all costs.

Like it or not, an increasing number of Americans are seeing cannabis as medicine. For this segment of the population, marijuana is not a bad thing. They view it as a lifesaving plant that has stopped their child's seizures or lessoned the symptoms of their ailments. Regardless of how you view marijuana or what stance you take, it is becoming a part of the mainstream culture in the United States.

The church historically has been divided on the subject of mainstream secular culture in general. Some embrace it and push Scripture aside. We see this today when a church or denomination embraces secular practices that God says should be shunned by believers. The early church struggled with this same kind of thing. Paul addressed this form of heresy within the Colossian church, warning them to not be deceived by the culture around them, which is contrary to the gospel of Christ.

Others swing to the other side of the pendulum and shun mainstream culture to the point of being standoffish and exclusive. Some take Paul's warning to the Colossian church as a warning to remove themselves from the outside world, and they may even unintentionally drift into isolation. The fear of being manipulated or swayed by the secular culture around the church takes over to push the Great Commandment and Great Commission aside.

A third category of Christians tries hard to balance the reality that we are called to minister to a people in a fallen world, but we are to be set apart from that world. It is impossible to walk this path in our fallen world without drifting from time to time. This group, which I believe is the largest, is willing to do the hard work of spreading the gospel in the midst of a culture hostile towards God.

The position one takes on culture and the church matters, because like it or not, the culture we live in cannot, and will not, be changed overnight. The truth is the mainstream, secular culture has a substantial effect on the church. It affects how we minister to the lost, live our lives and engage with God.

This makes it so important for the church to be informed about the secular culture and how it relates to Scripture. The only way to engage culture in a way that brings people to Christ, without sacrificing the essentials of the Christian faith in the process, is to first understand it. The debate surrounding marijuana is no different.

The time has come for the church to have a new conversation as cannabis laws change, instead of playing catch up after the fact. The body of Christ needs to be willing to have an open discussion with those who do not believe the same way they do about cannabis. The secular world is already having these discussions, so if the church is serious about making a difference where we live, work, and play, then it must join in the discussion, but in a way that glorifies Christ. It may not be easy, and will likely be uncomfortable, but it is essential to furthering the gospel message.

NOTHING NEW

It would be easy to believe the legalization of medical and recreational marijuana is something new. The reality is the law we have in the

United States making the cannabis plant illegal is a recent development. The low THC form of cannabis, known as hemp, was grown in the United States in the early 1600s as a vital crop. It was so vital that in 1619 Virginia required every farm in the colony to grow hemp.[1] They saw the hemp variant of the cannabis plant as essential for their survival. It provided rope, clothes, and ship sails for those brave enough to conquer the new world.

The problem is, when someone mentions cannabis, or marijuana, what comes to mind is not normally fabric and rope. If we are honest with ourselves, the first thing that comes to mind looks like a scene from a Cheech and Chong movie (you know what I'm talking about—or check it out online). The particular family of cannabis that most think of when they hear marijuana did not come to the United States on any large scale until the early 1900s.

In 1910 a revolution broke out in Mexico. As the war raged, citizens fled the death and destruction for the safety of the United States, bringing with them the high THC strains of the cannabis plant, which we refer to as marijuana. This influx of Mexican refugees brought about a new form of racism in this country. The fear of these refugees, and the plant they brought with them, eventually brought about the total prohibition of cannabis in the United States.

States began to pass laws criminalizing the use and possession of marijuana in the early 1930s after the end of prohibition. Then in 1937 the Marijuana Tax Act was passed by the federal government, which

---

1. Allison McNearney, "The Complicated History of Cannabis in the US," History.com, A&E Television Networks, April 20, 2018, https://www.history.com/news/marijuana-criminalization-reefer-madness-history-flashback.

made growing cannabis illegal unless the grower paid a hefty tax.[2] Farmers were still growing cannabis in the form of hemp in the US until 1970. When President Nixon signed the Controlled Substance Act into law, growing any form of the cannabis plant was federally banned until the Farm Bill of 2018 once again allowed farmers to grow industrial hemp.

The United States has seen the benefits of cannabis, specifically hemp, from the early days of the colonies. It has only been in the last hundred years as high THC marijuana strains have become more prevalent that our perspective on cannabis has changed. While individuals on both sides of the debate want to treat the push to legalize cannabis as if it is some new idea, it really is not. What we are seeing now is nothing more than a shift back to the view Americans held prior to the twentieth century.

THE CURRENT TREND

The shift in thinking that has brought us back to legalizing cannabis began in 1996, when California approved a measure that legalized marijuana for medicinal use. Numerous states have followed California's lead over the last twenty-four years in one form or another. A few states have acknowledged the benefits of the CBD found in cannabis and have passed laws allowing a hemp-grade CBD oil for medical use.

The main difference between marijuana and hemp is the amount of THC found in the plant. THC is the chemical that produces the "high" recreational users seek. By federal law, hemp cannot contain more than .3 percent THC by dry weight. While hemp is federally

---

2. Ibid.

legal, some states only allow CBD with no THC, where others follow the federal definition of hemp.

Things took a dramatic shift again in 2012. That year the people of Colorado, through popular vote, approved Amendment 64, which changed the state constitution to allow recreational marijuana. That same year Washington State voted to approved Initiative 502, legalizing recreational marijuana. In one year, the voters from two states initiated a drastic change in the way American's view marijuana. Soon other states followed suit.

The cultural shift did not stop there. In addition to the states that have legalized marijuana, several states have passed laws decriminalizing the possession of small amounts of the drug. Now, instead of arresting and charging people for possession of a controlled substance, as they have done for the last fifty years, states are looking the other way.

While they have not passed, laws have been introduced at the federal level to either legalize or to change what level of controlled substance cannabis is, similar to how opioids are handled. While the high THC form of cannabis is still illegal from a federal standpoint, the government has adopted the policy of not intervening in states where marijuana has been legalized by renewing the Rohrabacher–Farr Amendment[3] every year sense its passage in 2014.

All this points towards a return to a pre-twentieth century view on cannabis. The perception people have of this once-taboo plant are

---

3. The Rohrabacher-Farr Amendment is attached to spending bills and prohibits the Department of Justice from spending federal money to prevent states from implementing medical marijuana laws. https://www.thompsoncoburn.com/insights/blogs/tracking-cannabis/post/2017-05-31/interpreting-the-renewed-rohrabacher-farr-amendment-a-loophole-for-enforcement

changing. It is yet to be seen if this change is good or bad. Either way, change is happening across the country.

WHAT'S DRIVING THE CHANGE?

That is a complicated question. This shift in thinking cannot be narrowed down to one specific factor. I believe three factors are driving the change in marijuana laws around the country.

The mindset of the people plays a huge role in how government representatives see and react to cannabis. The last fifteen years have seen a fundamental shift in thinking. In 1969 only 12 percent of the American population believed in legalizing marijuana. By 2019 that number had risen to 67 percent.[4]

The change in thinking is not predominantly the result of one generation. While it may be tempting to think the hippie baby boomers of the 60s are driving this change in mindset, the reality is that millennials are actually leading the charge, but not by much. A 2019 poll by Pew Research found that 76 percent of the millennials surveyed supported cannabis legalization. The second largest percentage was Generation X at 65 percent supporting legalization. The baby boomer generation came in third with 63 percent in favor of legalization.[5]

Perhaps the biggest contributor to this new/old view on the cannabis plant is financial. The marijuana industry is turning out to be very,

4. Andrew Daniller, "Two-Thirds of Americans Support Marijuana Legalization," Pew Research Center, May 30, 2020, https://www.pewresearch.org/fact-tank/2019/11/14/americans-support -marijuana-legalization/.

5. Ibid.

very lucrative. In 2019, the total retail sales in the state of Colorado alone were a little over 1.75 billion dollars.[6]

It is not just the marijuana industry that benefits from these huge sales numbers. The financial benefits trickle through nearly every part of the economy. A vote to legalize cannabis, in any form, creates jobs in agriculture, manufacturing and sales. Unemployment goes down, which in turn frees up money for people to spend on restaurants, stores, and entertainment. As people find more disposable income, they encourage new businesses, which in turn further strengthens the economy.

The medical marijuana industry alone is projected to develop billions in income. Yes, you read that right. Billions with a *B*. Industry experts estimate the cannabis-based pharmaceutical industry, not counting the recreational marijuana sold in several states, will be a fifty-billion-dollar industry by 2029.[7] While that is a small drop in the bucket compared to what Americans spend on traditional pharmaceuticals, it's still an impressive number.

Right now you may be talking back to the book, or me, about how wrong that thinking is (unless I'm the only one who does that). Yes, legalization is not all good. Just as many say a lottery preys on the poor and uneducated, a similar thing can be said about legalizing marijuana. Full legalization takes the fear out of marijuana use for many. It also provides an easier way for addicts to get their fix. Only time will tell how much of an impact legalization has on these groups.

---

6. Tiney Ricciardi, "Colorado Marijuana Sales Hit a Record $1.75 Billion in 2019." In *The Denver Post*, February 18, 2020, https://www.denverpost.com/2020/02/18/colorado-marijuana-sales-2019/.

7. Dwight K. Blake, "Medical Marijuana Statistics - Guide - American Marijuana." In *American Marijuana*, July 29, 2021, https://americanmarijuana.org/medical-marijuana-statistics/.

I believe one more motivator is driving the legalization of both medical and recreational cannabis. This could arguably be the biggest incentive for states to pass cannabis reform: *taxes.*

There are no precedents for taxing marijuana. There is also little concern about competition from neighboring states or the internet. That leaves each state free to tax the growth, production, and sale of marijuana through whatever means and at whatever rate they choose to. With a large portion of that revenue coming from recreational sales in states like Colorado and Washington, few will ever complain if the state places exorbitant excise taxes on the growth, production, or sale of cannabis. That opens the door to potentially generate millions in untapped revenue for the state to use for various programs and services.

In the state of California that means a cultivation tax of $9.25 per ounce for flowers and $2.75 per ounce for leaves, then a 15 percent sales tax levied at the retail outlet. Colorado has a 15 percent tax when a grower sells to a retailer and another 15 percent sales tax when that retailer sells to the consumer. The tax is even higher in Washington State; a whopping 37 percent sales tax is placed on the sale of marijuana.[8]

The sales tax rates alone are impressive, but the total tax revenue the states collected in 2018 is even more impressive. Washington State collected 319 million dollars from marijuana taxes. California came in second with around 300 million in tax revenue. And Colorado came in third with 266.6 million dollars. After six years of legal marijuana sales in Colorado, the state has officially collected over one

---

8. Katherine Loughead and Morgan Scarboro, "How High Are Marijuana Taxes in Your State?" *Tax Foundation*, August 16, 2018, https://taxfoundation.org/state-marijuana-taxes-2018/.

billion dollars in tax revenue.[9] No matter what the initial motivation for legalizing marijuana is, the money certainly helps seal the deal.

One final factor drives the change in thinking. For many this is the greatest reason to legalize cannabis. Despite the negative connotation, the CBD in the cannabis plant has some health benefits. "As of February 3, 2022, thirty-seven states, three territories, and the District of Columbia allow the medical use of cannabis products."[10]

THE FEDERAL PERSPECTIVE

With more than half the states passing some form of medicinal cannabis law, one would wonder why cannabis is still illegal at the federal level. That's a good question and one that is difficult to narrow down a specific reason.

One reason the federal government has not made changes to cannabis laws is they cannot seem to agree on what reform should look like. Some Democrats are pushing for financial reforms that would allow cannabis businesses to operate as any other business does. Currently, banks and credit card companies are not able to work with cannabis businesses, creating a cash-only system. Other Democrats want full legalization of both recreation and medical use with minimal oversight at the federal level.

You will notice I haven't mentioned the Republican Party. While there are a few Republicans who are for cannabis reform, the majority seem

9. Felix Richter, "Infographic: Marijuana Brought in Millions in Tax Revenue Last Year." In *Statista Infographics*, March 27, 2019, https://www.statista.com/chart/17488/2018-tax-revenue-in-states-where-recreational-marijuana-use-is-legal/.

10. Karmen Hanson and Alise Garcia, State Medical Cannabis Laws, accessed July 13, 2022, https://www.ncsl.org/research/health/state-medical-marijuana-laws.aspx.

to be staunchly against it. Republican-controlled states are passing various cannabis laws, yet their federal representatives are reluctant to bring that reform to the nation. In a 2021 interview with Politico, two Republicans are quoted as admitting that "they don't support comprehensive federal cannabis reform, no matter what voters back home voted for."[11]

The financial aspect also comes into play just as it did with the move to legalize cannabis, at least at the federal level. As it stands now, the federal government has agreed to ignore the states where cannabis is now legal. In theory all sales are contained in individual states, so interstate commerce is not an issue. Legalization at the federal level could change that.

That change is concerning to many in the industry. Politico also notes that "Jennifer Canfield, a board member of the Alaska Marijuana Industry Association, says that federal legalization is supported by most voters in Alaska, but some in the state's industry would prefer legislation that does not throw the door wide open for a national cannabis market."[12]

Without some serious forethought, a law to legalize cannabis nationwide could create a mess of internet and interstate cannabis sales. Even states that continue to prohibit recreational cannabis could find themselves with an influx of internet sales. States like Washington, which has a 37 percent tax, could lose out to sales from states like Colorado where the tax rate is 30 percent. It also opens the door for issues with licensing, quality control, and general oversight of the industry.

---

11. Republicans Are Watching Their States Back Weed—and They're Not Sold," Politico, accessed July 14, 2022, https://www.politico.com/news/2021/06/27/republicans-weed-496390.

12. Ibid.

There is a lot to consider before sweeping cannabis reform can take place at the federal level. What it will look like and when it will happen is anyone's guess. Eventually the federal laws will change, but it will take time.

2

IN THE BEGINNING

Every new beginning comes from
some other beginning's end.

LUCIUS ANNAEUS SENECA

What is the first thing that comes to mind when you think of the stereotypical marijuana user?

Do you think of hippies living in a commune?

Perhaps a group of unruly teenagers.

Maybe images of wild parties and unkept misfits who are unable or unwilling to get a job.

There was a time when this stereotype may have been true. For nearly one hundred years marijuana was relegated to the outskirts of society. Cannabis use was synonymous with rebellion, laziness, and a gateway to heavy drug use. This is the picture the government, news media, and movies have painted of cannabis use. The question is whether or not that stereotype is still valid.

So let me ask the question again.

What is the first thing that comes to mind when you think of the stereotypical marijuana user?

Does your mind go to the family down the street who has a child with epilepsy?

What about the parent at your child's school who is fighting cancer?

Do you think about the soldier who bravely served their country only to face a lifetime of physical, mental, and emotional pain as a result?

How about the grandparent who is struggling with Alzheimer's?

For many, the first image that comes to mind of the stereotypical marijuana user looks more like the former group rather than the latter. Regardless of what we may think, as the perception of marijuana has changed in recent years, the face of the typical marijuana user has also changed. States like Colorado and California have moved the cannabis world from the back alleys and questionable nightclubs onto main street. The medicinal properties are pushing the cannabis plant into mainstream American life—and thus into the American church.

NOTHING NEW

God blessed King Solomon with the greatest gift a person can receive next to salvation. He asked for wisdom and God gave it. Thousands of years before the world began to debate the issue of medical marijuana, Solomon wrote,

What has been is what will be, and what has been done
is what will be done; there is nothing new under the sun.
Can one say about anything, "Look, this is new"? It has
already existed in the ages before us. (Ecclesiastes 1:9–10)

The wisest man to ever live knew there is nothing new under the sun.
He knew that what we see as new and innovative (or new and threatening), history sees as old and already done.

We tend to forget that fact. Human nature wants to treat things like
this as if they're new ideas, as if we're in uncharted waters. While
the cannabis discussion is new, uncharted territory for those of us in
the middle of the discussion today, it is still a rehashing of what was.
Instead of relying on history to guide the discussion, the conversation often overlooks, or is unaware of, the historical evidence and
attempts to reinvent the wheel.

MEDICAL ROOTS

Hemp has been grown around the world for thousands of years as a
food source, for rope production, and cloth. Archeologists in China
have discovered hemp was cultivated for its fibers as early as 2800 BC.[1]
It was only a matter of time before mankind began to find other uses
for the cannabis plant.

Less than seventy years later, the Chinese emperor Shen Neng introduced the world to the medicinal properties of cannabis. The Romans
discovered they could make a juice from the seeds that would cure
earaches. And the ancient Greek doctor, Galen, "used the drug to

1. "Hemp," Encyclopædia Britannica, Encyclopædia Britannica, inc., accessed January 28, 2022,
   https://www.britannica.com/plant/hemp.

treat pain and flatulence."[2] Cannabis was the go-to drug 4,600 years before the world had Advil and Gas-X.

Archeological evidence has even found cannabis in a young woman who died during childbirth outside of Jerusalem sometime around the third century AD.[3] Scientists believe the young mother may have been given cannabis during childbirth to ease pain and increase her contractions.[4] Doctors were using cannabis to assist during labor hundreds of years before the invention of epidurals and Pitocin.

THE FIRST GO-ROUND

In the United States the debate around medical marijuana rages as if this were unexplored virgin territory, as if doctors were discovering medical benefits of cannabis for the first time. Perhaps it would be more appropriate to say they are rediscovering the benefits of cannabis. The healing properties of medical marijuana have been known and put to use for years before the government made the plant illegal.

Medical marijuana was a common discussion among the medical community in the eighteenth and nineteenth centuries. In 1764 The New England Dispensatory suggested doctors use hemp roots to treat skin inflammation. The 1794 Edinburgh New Dispensary recommended

2. Mitch Earleywine, *Understanding Marijuana: A New Look at the Scientific Evidence* (Oxford: Oxford University Press, 2005) Kindle Edition, p. 11.

3. Joe Zlas, Harley Stark, Jon Seligman, Rina Levy, Ella Werker, Aviva Breuer, and Raphael Mechoulam, "Early Medical Use of Cannabis." In *Nature*, 363, no. 6426 (1993): 215–15, https://doi.org/10.1038/363215a0.

4. Mary Lynn Mathre, *Cannabis in Medical Practice: A Legal, Historical, and Pharmacological Overview of the Therapeutic Use of Marijuana* (Jefferson, NC: McFarland & Co.), 1997.

marijuana oil as a treatment for things like incontinence and venereal disease.[5]

In the 1860s the State Medical Society of Ohio gathered to discuss and list the uses cannabis had in the world of medicine. Their report noted medical marijuana was useful as a painkiller, could reduce inflammation, and help reduce coughs.[6] "The 1868 US Dispensatory listed numerous pages of medical uses for tincture of cannabis, an extract often formed by soaking marijuana in alcohol. The extract purportedly improved appetite, sexual interest, mental disorders, gout, cholera, hydrophobia, and insomnia."[7]

Long before the state of California legalized medical cannabis, American doctors were prescribing it for a long list of ailments. They took the time to research cannabis, the uses and routinely discussed it in professional settings. Before the invention of the chemical drugs doctors now rely on, medical professionals were using what God gave them.

THE DISCUSSION TODAY

While it is not a new subject, there are many developments which lead to a more complex argument, both for and against medical marijuana. Our modern, technologically advanced culture has pushed medical marijuana beyond a simple plant. Thousands of strains of cannabis have been specifically engineered to regulate the amount of THC and CBD found in the plant. Scientists are now able to genetically engineer a plant to target a specific ailment while reducing the

---

5. Earleywine, p. 13.

6. Tod H. Mikuriya, *Marijuana: Medical Papers, 1839–1972* (Oakland, CA: Medi-comp Press), 1973.

7. Earleywine, p. 14.

negative side effects. Medical marijuana has become a state-of-the-art industry that rivals the traditional pharmaceutical industry.

Individuals on both sides of the cannabis argument often are split on the subject, even within their own viewpoint. The anti-marijuana camp has people who are adamantly opposed to any-and-all forms legalization in this country. Others consider themselves anti-marijuana who are open to legalization as long as it is only in the context of medicinal use as prescribed by a doctor.

On the other side of the isle are those who consider themselves pro-marijuana. Some of those believe in full legalization with no government control, while others favor legalization with government oversight, similar to what we have in Colorado. You will also find individuals who consider themselves pro-marijuana, but insist it is only in the medicinal context, just as some of the anti-marijuana crowd does.

Even those in the limited legalization camp are often split on what that really means. Some insist the answer is removing cannabis from the controlled substance registry. Others are content to simply reschedule cannabis so it may be prescribed the same way doctors prescribe many other controlled substances. Strong opinions on both sides of the argument only make the discussion more complex and nearly impossible to navigate if we are not prepared.

3

THE MEDICAL ASPECT

[Marijuana] doesn't have a high potential for abuse,
and there are very legitimate medical applications. In
fact, sometimes marijuana is the only thing that works...

DR. SANJAY GUPTA, MD

Two main components of medical marijuana dominate the discussion; tetrahydrocannabinol, or THC, and cannabidiol, or CBD.

THC is the main psychoactive part of the cannabis plant. It is the substance that creates the high, which is what drives recreational users to marijuana. It does, however, appear to also play an important role when it comes to medical marijuana. THC has a tendency to increase the user's appetite while reducing nausea, making it ideal for cancer patients who are going through chemotherapy. It also plays a vital role in managing pain and inflammation. It may even be beneficial in addressing muscle control issues, such as those associated with Parkinson's or Huntington's disease.[1] CBD, on the other hand,

---

1. National Institute on Drug Abuse, "Is Marijuana Safe and Effective as Medicine?" National Institute on Drug Abuse, April 13, 2021, https://www.drugabuse.gov/publications/drugfacts/marijuana-medicine.

does not create the euphoric high associated with marijuana. But it can reduce pain and inflammation. It has also been shown to reduce epileptic seizures, along with helping those who suffer from various forms of mental illness and addiction problems.[2]

WHY DOES IT WORK?

The human body produces chemicals similar to cannabinoids. Scientists refer to them as endocannabinoids. It is thought that these chemicals work to help the human body cope with changes in our environment.[3] The body's endocannabinoid receptors "are present throughout the body, including our skin, immune cells, bone, fat tissue, liver, pancreas, skeletal muscle, heart, blood vessels, kidney, and gastrointestinal tract."[4] This results in the endocannabinoid system affecting things such as "pain, memory, mood, appetite, stress, sleep, metabolism, immune function, and reproductive function."[5] [6]

The part of the endocannabinoid system that plays a vital role in medical marijuana's effectiveness are the receptors. Scientists have labeled these CB1 and CB2. These receptors are found in the nervous system, with the CB1 receptors being primarily found in the central nervous system and the CB2 receptors primarily in the peripheral

2. Ibid.

3. Andrea Laurentiis, Hugo Araujo, and Valeria Rettori, "Role of the Endocannabinoid System in the Neuroendocrine Responses to Inflammation." In *Current Pharmaceutical Design* 20, no. 29 (2014): 4697–4706, https://doi.org/10.2174/1381612820666140130212957.

4. K. Mackie, "Cannabinoid Receptors: Where They Are and What They Do." In *Journal of Neuroendocrinology* 20, no. s1 (2008): 10–14, https://doi.org/10.1111/j.1365-2826.2008.01671.x.

5. Bradley E. Alger, "Getting High on the Endocannabinoid System," Cerebrum: The Dana Forum on Brain Science, The Dana Foundation, November 1, 2013, https://www.ncbi.nlm.nih.gov/pmc/articles/PMC3997295/.

6. Mauro Maccarrone, Itai Bab, Tamás Bíró, Guy A. Cabral, Sudhansu K. Dey, Vincenzo Di Marzo, Justin C. Konje, et al. "Endocannabinoid Signaling at the Periphery: 50 Years after THC." In *Trends in Pharmacological Sciences* 36, no. 5 (2015): 277–96, https://doi.org/10.1016/j.tips.2015.02.008.

system, including the immune cells of the body. The endocannabinoids can bind to either one of these receptors depending on where the body needs to be supported.[7]

The THC and CBD found in the cannabis plant interact with these receptors by mimicking the body's endocannabinoids. This makes it difficult to quantify the medicinal value of cannabis, as it may have a different interaction with the receptors depending on the individual. On top of that, both THC and CBD affect the body differently due to how they each interact with CB1 and CB2 receptors.

While THC will bind directly to either of the receptors, it tends to gravitate toward the CB1 receptors over the CB2. The attachment to the CB1 receptors is what causes the high most people associate with marijuana. When THC bonds with the CB2 receptors, the body does not experience as much of a strong physiological response.[8]

The THC found in the cannabis plant does more than cause the high people experience. It is also responsible for helping the body deal with pain and nausea. It works with the body to fight glaucoma and cancer. It also helps to alleviate the side effects many patients experience from cancer treatments, such as chemotherapy.[9]

CBD works just the opposite of THC. Where THC binds to the CB1 and CB2 receptors, CBD prevents chemicals such as THC from binding with the receptors in the body. This causes the CBD to work

7. Crystal Raypole, "Endocannabinoid System: A Simple Guide to How It Works." In *Healthline*, Healthline Media, May 17, 2019, https://www.healthline.com/health/endocannabinoid-system.

8. "Learn More about Cannabis, CBD, THC, & More: Marijuana Doctors: Online Medical Card Directory," Marijuana Doctors | Online Medical Card Directory, accessed January 28, 2022, https://www.marijuanadoctors.com/resources/endocannabinoid-system/.

9. Ibid.

on a physiological level instead of creating a psychological effect as THC does. CBD has the most effect on a specific endocannabinoid the body produces called anandamide, which has a chemical structure similar to THC. CBD "inhibits the FAAH enzyme that slows down and prevents anandamide breakdown." By controlling the FAAH enzyme, CBD allows anandamide to build up in the brain.[10] The human body needs a buildup of anandamide to stay regulated. Anandamide, known as the bliss molecule, plays a vital role in an individual's mental and physical health.[11]

CBD is an antipsychotic, a painkiller that works well with neuropathic pain and muscles spasms along with being an anti-anxiety agent. Studies have shown it to be effective in the treatment of inflammation, controlling tumor growth, PTSD, and epilepsy.[12]

A TEAM EFFORT

While both THC and CBD have positive effects on the human body, many believe the body gets the most benefit from a combination of the two. Natural hemp-based CBD oils, which contain less than 0.3 percent THC by law, can be more effective than the engineered oils that have no THC. Conditions like epilepsy may respond to a CBD-only oil, but in some cases the patient needs a dose of THC to make the most impact.

This is where things get touchy. Many of the states that do not allow medical marijuana have passed laws regulating CBD oil. They only allow products that do not contain THC to be sold. While CBD-only

---

10. Ibid.

11. Patrick Alban, "Anandamide: Bliss Molecule for Happiness & Mental Balance," Be Brain Fit, September 1, 2021, https://bebrainfit.com/anandamide/.

12. "Learn More about Cannabis, CBD, THC, & More."

products may benefit some, many individuals would benefit from a low dose of THC.

Laws like this make it more difficult to understand how effective cannabis may or may not be. One person may respond well to a CBD-only supplement while another person may not. It does not mean cannabis only works half the time; rather, it means that half the patients may need some THC to respond favorably.

A BALANCING ACT

The human body is a complex machine. God designed our bodies with a system of checks and balances to keep us healthy, but due to numerous factors, things get out of balance. One of those systems that tends to become unbalanced is the endocannabinoid system. Recreational marijuana use introduces an increase in THC, which causes the body to overload the CB1 and CB2 receptors. This causes the high feeling and can lead to serious complications for people who are allergic to cannabis.

At other times the body may not produce enough endocannabinoids to maintain the necessary systems, such as inflammation control and natural immunity. Sometimes the body may not have enough CB1 or CB2 receptors. The theory on this is called Clinical Endocannabinoid Deficiency. When the human body does not produce enough endocannabinoids, or is lacking receptors, the system becomes unbalanced. This imbalance may explain why some people develop conditions such as

- Fibromyalgia
- Irritable Bowel Syndrome (IBS)

- Migraines
- Alzheimer's
- Parkinson's

Researchers have found that people with these conditions have lower endocannabinoid levels than those who are not afflicted with the disease.[13] While this is still a theory in need of more testing, Clinical Endocannabinoid Deficiency could explain why cannabis works so well in the treatment of a multitude of illnesses.

MORE WORK TO DO

There is still a lot we do not know about medical marijuana and how it interacts with the human body. Unfortunately, we have a limited amount of test data, at least here in the United States. The big problem right now is that very few organizations can perform the needed studies because marijuana in any form is, at the time this was written, federally illegal.

Any scientist who wants to do a medical marijuana study must get approval from the DEA and the FDA. Those who have gone through the approval process end up with less than 200 participants, which will call into question the findings.[14] More research is needed to determine if the medicinal claims are justified, but at this time it is counterproductive to spend millions for such low results.

---

13. Ethan B. Russo, "Clinical Endocannabinoid Deficiency Reconsidered: Current Research Supports the Theory in Migraine, Fibromyalgia, Irritable Bowel, and Other Treatment-Resistant Syndromes," Cannabis and cannabinoid research, Mary Ann Liebert, Inc., July 1, 2016, https://www.ncbi.nlm.nih.gov/pmc/articles/PMC5576607/.

14. Bara. Vaida, "Results of Marijuana Research," WebMD, accessed January 28, 2022, https://www.webmd.com/pain-management/features/medical-marijuana-research-web#2.

While widespread testing is limited, there have been a few break-throughs in the United States. As of 2020, the FDA has approved one drug derived from cannabis. Epidiolex is a pure CBD oil that contains 0 percent THC and is currently only approved to treat two specific forms of epilepsy, Dravet Syndrome and Lennox-Gastaut Syndrome, in children over the age of two.[15]

Scientist have also developed three drugs based on synthetic forms of THC that have been FDA approved. These drugs are being used for cancer patients who are going through chemotherapy. While these drugs are not cannabis, they are a chemical equivalent of it and work within the human body in similar ways to cannabis.

The lack of testing makes it difficult to distinguish fact from fiction. Medical professionals do not have the facts and data they need, which often produces skepticism in portions of the medical community, especially when discussing the potential side effects of cannabis.

---

15. Office of the Commissioner, "FDA and Cannabis: Research and Drug Approval Process," U.S. Food and Drug Administration, FDA, accessed January 28, 2022, https://www.fda.gov/news-events/public-health-focus/fda-and-cannabis-research-and-drug-approval-process.

4

THE ADDICTION ASPECT

There are many drugs that have many serious side effects and that are harmful to people. Marijuana is no different than that. And especially we should try to discourage young people from using marijuana.

DANA ROHRABACHER

We have looked at the medical aspect of cannabis, so now our attention turns to reasons an individual has for being anti-cannabis.

While the war on cannabis began in the early twentieth century, it really gained momentum in the 1970s and 80s. In 1971 President Richard Nixon placed cannabis on the Controlled Substance Act until studies would be done. Then in 1972 Attorney General John Mitchell permanently put cannabis on the controlled list, as a schedule one drug even though the studies did not support this action.[1]

If you are not familiar with the Controlled Substance Act, the federal government has created a list of drugs they have deemed to be

---

1. David Downs, "The Science behind the DEA's Long War on Marijuana." In *Scientific American*, April 19, 2016, https://www.scientificamerican.com/article/the-science-behind -the-dea-s-long-war-on-marijuana/.

a controlled substance based on several factors. "Drugs, substances, and certain chemicals used to make drugs are classified into five (5) distinct categories or schedules depending upon the drug's acceptable medical use and the drug's abuse or dependency potential."[2]

Have you ever gotten a prescription for which you must show identification and sign additional forms? If you have, your doctor has prescribed a controlled substance. Cold medicines containing pseudoephedrine are not controlled substances but are regulated due to their being used in making a controlled substance.

The table below gives a description of each schedule and examples of the drugs within that schedule.

	Description	Examples
Schedule I	Substances or chemicals with a high potential for abuse and no medicinal uses	Heroin LSD Ecstasy Marijuana
Schedule II	Substances, or chemicals with a high potential for abuse, may have severe dependence	Vicodin Cocaine OxyContin Fentanyl Opium
Schedule III	Substances, or chemicals with a moderate or low dependence	Tylenol with codeine Steroids Testosterone

2. "Drug Scheduling," DEA, accessed July 26, 2022, https://www.dea.gov/drug-information/drug-scheduling.

	Description	Examples
Schedule IV	Substances, or chemicals with a low potential for abuse or dependence	Xanax Valium Diazepam Ambient
Schedule V	Substances, or chemicals with a lower potential for abuse than schedule IV and contain limited narcotics	Robitussin AC Lomotil Motofen Lyrica
https://www.dea.gov/drug-information/drug-scheduling		

THE SHORT TERM

For a recreational cannabis user, the effects are felt within minutes if the drug is smoked, and they last for two-to-four hours. If the user consumes the marijuana in an edible form, the effects will take one-to-two hours to take effect and can last for eight hours or more.[3] This makes the negative short-term effects of cannabis as much of a concern as the long-term effects.

When the THC attaches to the CB1 receptors, the user experiences the high associated with marijuana use. The user may also experience things such as

- altered senses (for example, seeing brighter colors)
- altered sense of time
- changes in mood

---

3. Mitch Kline, "How to Dose Edibles," Maggie's Farm Marijuana Dispensaries, September 30, 2021, https://maggiesfarmmarijuana.com/how-to-dose-edibles/.

- impaired body movement
- difficulty with thinking and problem-solving
- impaired memory
- hallucinations (when taken in high doses)
- delusions (when taken in high doses)
- psychosis (risk is highest with regular use of high potency marijuana)[4]

These short-term effects will vary from individual to individual. For those who have an allergy to the cannabis plant, these side effects may be more severe. If a person experiences these side effects, the amount of marijuana consumed will also make a difference in how severe the reactions are.

Some of the short-term effects of cannabis use are similar to alcohol use. Users may have difficulty in walking, driving, thinking rationally, and coordination. Anyone who has spent time watching people leave a bar or beer tent has seen these same things. When a cannabis user chooses to drive or operate machinery, these impairments create a safety hazard just as alcohol does.

THE LONG TERM

The long-term effects of cannabis use are more difficult to define, as we circle back to the lack of test data, at least here in the United States. There are a few studies that provide some basis to be concerned about the effects of long-term cannabis abuse.

---

4. "Cannabis (Marijuana) Drugfacts," National Institutes of Health, U.S. Department of Health and Human Services, March 22, 2022, https://nida.nih.gov/publications/drugfacts/cannabis-marijuana.

There appears to be a correlation between the age a person first begins to abuse marijuana and the number of issues they may face later in life. A teen or pre-teen's brain is still developing and, as a result, may be more susceptible to the negative effects. This may include a higher risk of dropping out of school, lower IQs, depression and anxiety. There are also studies that link early cannabis abuse to disrupted brain development.[5]

Duke University participated in a study on cannabis in New Zealand. This study found that individuals who abused marijuana as teenagers and continued to heavily use it as adults had lost, on average eight IQ points between the ages of thirteen and thirty-eight, where those who began cannabis use as adults did not show a noticeable decline. The lost mental abilities the former group experienced did not return after they ceased abusing marijuana.[6]

THE GATEWAY DRUG

Most people reading this have heard parents, teachers, and police officers talk about how marijuana is a gateway drug. That has been the push for many years in the attempt to control illegal drug use. But is it true?

Maybe, but not necessarily.

Studies done on animals have noticed a possible connection between THC and other drug use. Young rodents that have been given THC

---

5. Jennifer Casarella, "The Long-Term Side Effects of Marijuana Use," WebMD, accessed July 26, 2022, https://www.webmd.com/connect-to-care/addiction-treatment-recovery/marijuana/long-term-effects-marijuana-use.

6. "Cannabis (Marijuana) Drugfacts," https://nida.nih.gov/publications/drugfacts/cannabis-marijuana.

tend to have a greater response in the area of the brain that controls rewards when other drugs are introduced.[7]

However, the majority of individuals who use cannabis do not go on to abuse other drugs. It happens, but is not as widespread as we were once led to believe. Often, those who do have some other factor that leads to a higher risk of dependency or addiction to those drugs. While they may have used marijuana at an early age, it may not be the cause of the dependency, instead a symptom.[8]

The cannabis discussion can be tense regardless of what side of the debate you fall on. For Christians, the debate should be entered prayerfully and with grace. We should also be mindful of the most important question in this whole debate: What does the Bible have to say?

---

7. Ibid.

8. "Risk of Using Other Drugs," Centers for Disease Control and Prevention, October 19, 2020, https://www.cdc.gov/marijuana/health-effects/risk-of-other-drugs.html.

5

CANNABIS AND SCRIPTURE

God also said, "Look, I have given you every
seed-bearing plant on the surface of the entire
earth and every tree whose fruit contains seed.

GENESIS 1:29

And don't get drunk with wine, which leads to
reckless living, but be filled by the Spirit.

EPHESIANS 5:18

The subject of cannabis is not a cut-and-dried issue. Perhaps it would be less of a volatile subject if Jesus had said, "Thou shalt not smoke the wacky tobbacy" or if Paul had told Timothy to occasionally have a toke for his ailments.

Okay, so that may be a little crude. However, crude or not, the reality is that neither of those statements, nor anything close to them, can be found in the pages of Scripture. Out of all sixty-six books of the Bible, what we consider controversial medication is never discussed. The closest example one could point to would be 1 Timothy 5:23 where Paul tells Timothy, "Don't continue drinking only water, but use a little wine because of your stomach and your frequent illnesses."

In that verse Paul instructed Timothy to take advantage of the medic-inal properties of wine for what ailed him. Paul, perhaps even under the guidance of Luke the physician, advised Timothy to use wine as a medicine. Modern studies have found that red wine may reduce the amount of bad bacteria in a person's stomach, which is known to cause stomach ulcers.[1] Alcohol is also known to kill germs and bac-teria that can be present in untreated water, as would have been the case in the first century AD.

He was not, however, condoning drunkenness. While this verse does not say this, when we look at this statement in the larger context of the Bible, the intent was to use it sparingly, not overindulging. Paul realized there are medicinal uses for wine, and he wanted his young protégé to take full advantage of those properties so he could serve the Lord to his fullest potential.

THE PITFALL

This passage in the Bible is a prime example of the pit we tend to fall into in the church. A staunch teetotaler, for instance, might say the wine is not wine like we have (which is likely true) or that wine in the Bible is really grape juice. Some would say wine is okay, but beer is not, because Paul specifically said wine. Others would insist this passage removes any and all prohibition on alcohol.

The reality is that all three of these views are wrong. The second could have some merit, although it is a bit of a stretch. When we look at the larger picture of Scripture, we see the wine of the Bible was a fermented drink, likely done as a method of preservation. It had an

---

1. Daniel J. DeNoon, "With Beer or Wine, the Stomach's Fine," WebMD, December 30, 2002, https://www.webmd.com/heartburn-gerd/news/20021230/with-beer-wine-stomachs-fine.

alcohol content, and it was not thought of as bad and was not universally condemned. We also see that drunkenness is prohibited and this passage does not nullify that command.

CONVICTION OR COMMAND?

Too often we let our personal convictions become universal commands. Here's what I mean. There is nothing wrong or sinful for a person to be convicted by the Holy Spirit that drinking alcohol in any form is wrong. By the same token, it is not wrong or sinful for a person to be convicted by that same Holy Spirit that having a glass of wine or beer is perfectly acceptable.

The sinful act comes when a person takes their personal, Holy Spirit-given convictions on things where the Bible is ambiguous and attempts to turn them into universal commands of Scripture. Christians can have different convictions on the gray areas of Scripture, and most of the time neither one is wrong. These personal revelations are just that, personal. They are not universal revelations to be put on the same level as what God reveals through His written Word.

We are wrong, however, when we put aside the convictions of the Spirit for the convictions of man. If the Spirit convicts you to drink or not to drink, and then you do the opposite based on the guidance of a friend or pastor, you have just sinned. Somewhere along the line we have lost the ability to understand, and preach, grace in the gray areas of Scripture. Part of making disciples is creating individuals who can, and will, think rationally about a topic and then filter everything through the lens of Scripture.

As such, discussions like those we are about to embark on often go awry, ending in damaged relationships with both God and man. As we move forward, I encourage you to keep an open mind. Please understand, my goal is to present the facts along with both sides of the argument. I encourage you to be secure in what the Lord has convicted you of, so much so that you are able to hear, and I mean really hear, the other side.

The journey to hearing and understanding those who do not believe as we do begins with Scripture. We as Christians must be willing to read the Word of God with an open mind and open heart. As we read, listen to, and teach the Word of God, we must be open to let the Holy Spirit lead us into a proper understanding of Scripture. This means being open to the idea that what we believe and hold dear may be wrong. It is easy to read the Bible through the lens of what we believe is true instead of looking for what God says is true.

CONFIDENT AND TEACHABLE

One of the greatest tactics Satan uses to destroy the church today is through our hard-heartedness. It is human nature to fear being wrong, especially in the United States. We have a culture that is quick to destroy others for mistakes, which only fuels the inability to have these types of discussions. An individual's failure to admit, or even accept, when they are wrong creates a spirit that is not teachable.

Of course, the best way to defeat the fear is to really know what we claim to believe. We must own our hope and salvation. When we are confident that what we believe and know to be true comes from Scripture, it is okay to listen to opposing viewpoints. We can discuss our views instead of arguing our point. It is that maturity in Christ that allows the church to agree to disagree on things where Scripture is not explicit, and stand firm where it is. We as American Christians often make universal truths where God allows freedom and thus die on crosses God never intended for us to.

The goal in this and every hard discussion should be to build, not burn, bridges. Bridge building is hard work that takes time, energy, and a willingness to submit completely to the Lord. The end result is to create a church environment filled with understanding, compassion, and unity, one that is attractive to those on the outside looking in. Those are the environments where Jesus is evident in all that is said and done.

Hard work has its rewards. When that hard work is building bridges to the lost or creating unity in the body of Christ, the payoff is far beyond what we could ever imagine. God can do anything through, and sometimes in spite of, us. The work is a lot more attractive when it is done by people who genuinely love one another.

Perhaps the best way to end this chapter is to reflect on Paul's words to the Corinthian church:

> Love is patient, love is kind. Love does not envy, is not boastful, is not arrogant, is not rude, is not self-seeking, is not irritable, and does not keep a record of wrongs. Love finds no joy in unrighteousness but rejoices in the truth. It bears all things, believes all things, hopes all things, endures all things. (1 Corinthians 13:4–7)

6

KIND OF? SORT OF? MAYBE? ... NOT

*"Everything is permissible for me," but not everything
is beneficial. "Everything is permissible for me,"
but I will not be mastered by anything.*

1 CORINTHIANS 6:12

*"Everything is permissible," but not everything is beneficial.
"Everything is permissible," but not everything builds up.*

1 CORINTHIANS 10:23

Context is key in most things we say and do in this life. One cannot accurately read and interpret Scripture apart from the context of the entire passage or book. Many well-intentioned people go astray because they take the Word of God out of context. It is easy to find passages to support our beliefs if we look solely at one line or phrase.

A failure to look at or understand the context is not limited to Scripture alone. How often do we see one group who explodes over a word or phrase they found offensive, only to see it in the proper context and realize it was never meant that way. It is impossible to understand the true meaning if we do not know, or care about, the context in which it was delivered.

We as human beings, and Americans in particular, tend to get upset at the slightest things. We seem to be looking to be offended instead of looking to understand one another. One prime example is an artist who released a song that set part of the special needs/disability community into a fury. She used a single word that a portion of the community found offensive and was triggered by. In the context of the song, it was perfectly acceptable and never once was directed towards an individual with a disability. Yet a portion of the people were outraged.

When we wear our emotions on our sleeves, it is impossible to determine, or care about, the context. We spend our life coiled to strike at the slightest hint that we could be offended. There is nothing Christ honoring about a life lived this way, yet the church is full of people who are just looking to be offended. Imagine the revival that could take place if we spent as much time expecting God to move mountains as we do expecting to be offended by grains of sand.

Every person has a desire to be heard and respected. Often the radical reactions to people and things stems from this desire. The irony is the more we blow up and scream our point, the less people respect, or care, about what we have to say. In the end we just look foolish as we scream at each another.

Jesus calls us, His followers, to something more, something better. Scripture may not specifically spell out the answer to all our problems, but it does spell out how to handle them. We have a treasure trove of wisdom in the pages of the Bible. All we have to do is read it with a heart and mind looking for God to lead.

A UNIQUE TITLE

I started this chapter with a unique title, and I'll explain it before we move on. I hit a wall with this book. I wanted to look at some Scripture references people could use to defend the views they hold on cannabis, but I was struggling with how to get there.

In my quiet time this year I have been reading through the Bible. I reached the book of Job, which is one of my favorites. When we entered the life of special needs parents, Job was my comfort. And as usual, Job did not disappoint.

One morning I was reading chapters 28–32, where Job is defending his righteousness. David was called a man after God's own heart, but Job certainly fit that bill long before David was born. In the middle of this, the Holy Spirit gave me the title of this chapter: Kind of? Sort of? Maybe?

If we are all honest, these are questions we all ask ourselves, or should, from time to time. This is particularly important when we find a passage of Scripture that backs up our opinions on controversial topics. The reality is that the answer to these questions might be NOT. But we miss it, especially if we never question why we believe what we do about a particular topic.

One key part of being a mature Christian is how we approach Scripture. Do we go to the Word of God looking to confirm our opinions? Or do we go to the Word of God to define our opinions? There is a huge difference between the two. One seeks to make the Bible fit what they believe, while the other seeks to make what they believe fit the Bible.

As we look at some of the passages used to defend or deny cannabis use, I encourage you to take a moment and do a heart check. When you go to Scripture, are you looking for God to lead you to His conclusion? Are you on edge, waiting to be offended, or are you expecting the Holy Spirit to teach?

> Lord, send the Holy Spirit to lead, teach and rebuke as we move forward. Lead us to Your conclusion and Your will in this discussion. Guide us to the place where our opinions become Yours. May Your will be done on earth as it is in Heaven. Amen

IN THE BEGINNING

The story of life on earth begins with the book of Genesis, so it is fitting that we began our look at the Word of God there. Long before the first recorded use of cannabis, Moses was recording the story of creation.

> God also said, "Look, I have given you every seed-bearing plant on the surface of the entire earth and every tree whose fruit contains seed. This will be food for you, for all the wildlife of the earth, for every bird of the sky, and for every creature that crawls on the earth—everything having the breath of life in it—I have given every green plant for food." And it was so. God saw all that he had made, and it was very good indeed. (Genesis 1:29–31)

There it is! Every green plant is good for food, so it should be okay for other uses, right? Time to close the book. Discussion over!

Yeah, not so fast. Two chapters later Moses wrote:

And he said to the man, "Because you listened to your
wife and ate from the tree about which I commanded
you, 'Do not eat from it': The ground is cursed because
of you. You will eat from it by means of painful labor all
the days of your life. It will produce thorns and thistles
for you, and you will eat the plants of the field. (Genesis 3:17–18)

So that is it! The ground is cursed so, by extension, plants like the
cannabis plant are a result of that. Anything cursed is bad!

Sorry, you need to reign in that enthusiasm.

This is the tension we must navigate when having a discussion that is
as controversial in the church world as cannabis is. One person can
certainly point to Genesis 1 as justification for cannabis use. Others will look at this passage and insist it only applies to hemp seeds,
which are edible. Some might even say cannabis is okay as long as it
is made into something edible and, yes, that is a real thing not just
a sitcom gag.

Then we get to Genesis 3, where God pronounced the ground cursed.
It would be easy to say this includes plants like cannabis. Some will
insist the cannabis plant we know is not what God intended, and
while the Garden of Eden version was okay, what we have now is
not. Others could insist cannabis did not exist in the garden. Instead,
God created it as part of the cursed earth after the fall.

So what is the correct interpretation?

How are we to know which one is right?

PERMISSIBLE OR NOT?

Perhaps the New Testament will straighten out this issue. Let's look at what could be the greatest argument for the use of cannabis in any form we can find in all of Scripture. The Apostle Paul wrote to the church in Corinth because there were some substantial sin issues among their ranks. He wrote:

> "Everything is permissible for me," but not everything is beneficial. "Everything is permissible for me," but I will not be mastered by anything. (1 Corinthians 6:12)

Four chapters late he reminded the Corinthians:

> "Everything is permissible," but not everything is beneficial. "Everything is permissible," but not everything builds up. (1 Corinthians 10:23)

So, what do we do with this? It would be easy to look at this passage and insist cannabis is permissible. After all, that is what Paul said. It's right there in black and white. Everything is permissible for us. He even said it twice in each passage!

What do we do with the second half of the first sentence? Everything is permissible, but not everything is beneficial. We could say the THC found in full marijuana is not beneficial and thus cannabis is not permissible. There is also the argument that cannabis can become a master (just like money, food, or alcohol) and that Paul insisted he, and we, should not be mastered by anything other than Christ.

This is where it gets difficult. How do we define beneficial?

Merriam Webster defines beneficial as "producing good results or helpful effects: conferring benefits."[1] Based on studies done around the world, we know cannabis has some medicinal properties. We know it stops or reduces seizures. It helps many around the world and thus, by Merriam Webster's definition, it would be beneficial.

Some would argue it is not. The idea that the bad outweighs the good may determine the definition of beneficial for some people. Is it beneficial if it leads even one person into sin? It is hard to overlook the bad when we cannot quantify the amount of good cannabis does or is able to do.

Then we get into how many need to see positive results for something to be defined as beneficial. Is it five? Ten? A hundred? One person may set their preferred number at ten where another sets it at 100,000.

How do we come to a consensus on an objective number?

CLEAR AS MUD

Welcome to the world of biblical ambiguity! Along with many other issues, this one is not completely clear. Scripture gives enough information to provide us with a starting point for the Holy Spirit to lead us into a personal conviction. And it is just that, a personal conviction. There are some things God seems to want us to wrestle with and ultimately come to a conclusion where we have to agree to disagree for the good of the body of Christ.

---

1. "Beneficial Definition & Meaning," Merriam-Webster, accessed July 2, 2022, https://www.merriam-webster.com/dictionary/beneficial.

Scripture cannot, and will not, contradict itself. We as created beings on the other hand can and often do. I could write an entire book on Scripture verses we use to justify one position or another on cannabis. It still does not change the fact that the Bible is silent on the subject.

We can look at numerous passages which give us guidance for living the Christian life. While these provide a road map to get to the destination, ultimately there are multiple routes one could take to that destination.

If Scripture is not clear on this issue, why do we carry on like it is?

7

THE WEAKER BROTHER

Welcome anyone who is weak in faith,
but don't argue about disputed matters.

ROMANS 14:1

You cannot reason people out of a position
that they did not reason themselves into.

BEN GOLDACRE

In many churches and Christian circles, people are ready to condemn any, and all, actions they deem wrong. In some respects this is not wrong thinking. Paul was quick to correct the sinful actions many churches were falling into at the time. There is certainly a Biblical mandate to correct other believers so they do not fall into the hands of Satan. As we have seen in the previous chapter, when it comes to cannabis, the definition of sinful actions is open to interpretation.

There is a mandate in the Bible I firmly believe should govern this discussion. In the fourteenth chapter of Romans, Paul lays out the law of liberty and the law of love. This one chapter of Scripture provides an instruction manual for entering into any kind of touchy discussion where the parties do not believe the same thing. We may have liberty, but that liberty never trumps love.

How often do you read Romans 14 before having a discussion about cannabis?

Before we dig into this chapter, I want to state this may seem like it is a one-sided conversation. It may seem that I am coming down on one camp over the other. I assure you that is not my intention. This is, after all, a two-way street. Paul was writing to the church, both then and now. Regardless of which side of the debate we fall on, this is something all Christians need to read and take to heart.

THE LAW OF LIBERTY

By the time you get to Romans chapter 14, Paul is not pulling any punches. He dives right into the heart of the matter, writing,

> Welcome anyone who is weak in faith, but don't argue about disputed matters. One person believes he may eat anything, while one who is weak eats only vegetables. One who eats must not look down on one who does not eat, and one who does not eat must not judge one who does, because God has accepted him. Who are you to judge another's household servant? Before his own Lord he stands or falls. And he will stand, because the Lord is able to make him stand....
>
> But you, why do you judge your brother or sister? Or you, why do you despise your brother or sister? For we will all stand before the judgment seat of God. For it is written, *As I live, says the Lord, every knee will bow to me, and every*

tongue will give praise to God. So then, each of us will give
an account of himself to God. (Romans 14:1–4, 10–12)

Wow, what a slap in the face!

Paul makes it clear: We have liberty in Christ. As he told the church in
Corinth, this is the same liberty that makes all things permissible but
not all things beneficial. The Romans may have understood this but
took it one step too far. That is, some in the church apparently understood and enjoyed the liberty they had, but they were holding it over
the heads of those who did not see it the same way. And even though
Paul does not say it, the sentiment likely flowed the other way as well.

Sound familiar?

Paul cut to the quick in verses 10–12. He called out their judgment of
the weaker brother and sister, asking why they despised other Christians. Harsh, but a much-needed reminder. When we get on our self-
righteous horses and judge other Christians, we despise them. That
judgment makes them less than us and perverts our view of God and
His creation. It inflates our pride and gives Satan a foothold with
which to destroy us and the church.

THE CANNABIS CONVERSATION

I do not believe most Christians go into a conversation with the intentional thought that they are the stronger believer. However, the sub-
conscious often leads the conversation in that direction. Regardless
of the subject matter, the idea is that one person is a stronger Christian than the other because of what they believe on the subject. The
problem is that both sides typically think this way.

The cannabis discussion is no different. It might actually be worse than other discussions. The pro-cannabis crowd is full of parents who see it as medicine for themselves or their kids. This creates an emotionally charged situation. Those emotions, intentional or unintentional, create a need to win at all costs mentality. The permissible aspect of liberty in Christ overrules all else. It is very easy to see how this side sees the other as the weaker brother.

Those on the other side of the discussion can feel like the stronger Christians because their view is often the consensus of the church they attend. If everyone believes like you, how can you be wrong? That is a dangerous way to think. Cults form and thrive on that kind of logic.

It is not long before emotions come into play. And it is easy to feel superior, even if we do not intend to, when those who do not believe as we do melt down. Obviously the one who keeps their cool and tries to have a rational conversation is the stronger Christian, right?

Not necessarily.

When you encounter those situations, did you hear what the other person was saying? Can you repeat their point to another person? If the answer is no, both sides have failed.

The judgment Paul warned about can take many forms. Sometimes it shows up as a refusal to have a conversation; other times it appears in how we speak to those who disagree with us. Do we talk *to* the person or *at* them? Do we see those we disagree with as people who have worth and deserve to be heard?

Thankfully there is a solution to this issue.

THE LAW OF LOVE

Paul issues a straightforward command, "Therefore, let us no longer judge one another. Instead decide never to put a stumbling block or pitfall in the way of your brother or sister" (Romans 14:13). I do not think he could have made it any clearer: Stop judging one another!

The second half of the verse is the most important for our discussion. Paul tells the church to deliberately do everything we can to keep from causing a brother or sister to stumble in their walk with Jesus.

That does not mean we are guilty of sin if someone stumbles because of us while we do everything possible to avoid it. What Paul means is we should go out of our way to lift up one another by not doing or saying things that would cause them to stumble.

This can be difficult because we cannot always point to specific actions that would be stumbling blocks. For a recovering alcoholic, seeing you have a beer with a meal could be a stumbling block. For the alcoholic who has not yet admitted their addiction, seeing you have a beer could be the moment they are freed from the guilt and shame associated with a teetotaler upbringing. One person stumbles while another finds Jesus. One simple act with two separate outcomes.

When we talk about cannabis, do we cause another to stumble? Does our conversation draw people closer to Christ or drive them away? Both sides of the argument are guilty of causing the other to stumble. One may be driven to anger and harsh words, while the other is driven from church. Either way, the Kingdom loses.

Paul has the solution to this issue. "So then, let us pursue what promotes peace and what builds up one another" (Romans 14:19). The goal is to have this discussion in a way that introduces the lost to the Savior while promoting peace among the body of Christ. This is not an easy task and can go awry very quickly if we are not careful.

The key is to listen more than we speak. Know, and be confident of, your convictions. But also be mindful of what it takes to bring about peace in the church. Sometimes the only way to accomplish this is follow Paul's advice of "whatever you believe about these things, keep between yourself and God" (Romans 14:22).

If our discussion is not civil, it is time to table it until the Holy Spirit can lead us through it in a Christ-honoring way. We have an obligation to the Lord to let Him lead in His time and will. "Let your speech always be gracious, seasoned with salt, so that you may know how you should answer each person" (Colossians 4:6). Sometimes that means we should not answer, as listening is often the most gracious thing we can do for a person who desperately needs Jesus.

A DRUNKEN TEMPLE

*Bottom line, your body is a temple, and you have
to treat it that way. That's how God designed it.*

RAY LEWIS

*Your body is not a temple, it's an amusement park.
Enjoy the ride.*

ANTHONY BOURDAIN

n his letter to the church at Corinth, Paul attempted to set them
straight regarding some of the sins they had fallen into. In the process he wrote one of the most used, and misused, lines in Scripture
to condemn things like smoking, drinking, and cannabis use. In the
proper context, Paul was condemning the sexual immorality running
rampant in the Corinthian church. Paul wrote,

> Don't you know that your body is a temple of the Holy
> Spirit who is in you, whom you have from God? You are
> not your own, for you were bought at a price. So glorify
> God with your body. (1 Corinthians 6:19–20)

The question becomes, is it appropriate to use this verse to condemn
anything other than sexual immorality? I would assert there is an

underlying principle found here that goes beyond sexual sin. Our bodies are a dwelling place for the Holy Spirit and were created in the image of God, which we see in Genesis 1:27.

THE PERFECT TEMPLE

What defines a body that is a perfect temple, one that glorifies God to the fullest?

A previous pastor and friend of mine would often quote the popular Christian saying, "I don't smoke, drink, or chew or go with girls who do." Is this the epitome of a perfect temple for the Spirit to dwell in? Some would say yes.

We know the health risks associated with smoking and chewing tobacco. Even though alcohol has some medicinal properties, excessive use leads to all kinds of problems. So why not lump cannabis into this group?

It would be fair to say that smoking marijuana has the potential to damage the body. While we do not have good scientific studies on the effects of long-term cannabis use, we know inhaling smoke is detrimental to the human body. The effects of inhaling secondhand smoke kills more than 41,000 Americans each year.[1]

It is easy to point to these things and insist that if we cut them out, we have a body worthy of being called a temple. If only it were that simple. How often do we turn on the TV to see an overweight pastor,

---

1. "Health Effects of Secondhand Smoke," American Lung Association, accessed July 13, 2022, https://www.lung.org/quit-smoking/smoking-facts/health-effects/secondhand-smoke.

doctor, or politician telling us how bad something is while ignoring the obesity health crisis they embody?

What about the food you eat? Is it all natural? Does it contain preservatives or artificial substances? Is it always healthy? Probably not. In our modern world it is nearly impossible to remove the bad substances from our diets. Some try, while others do not.

It is hard to use this verse to justify an anti-cannabis position without looking like a hypocrite. I know I certainly could not.

I DID NOT INHALE

That line, made famous by the former President Bill Clinton, brings up another argument countering the body-as-a-temple argument. There could be a reasonable argument made that as long as cannabis is not smoked, it is not detrimental to the body and thus, is not bad. As we discussed earlier, there are medicinal benefits to cannabis. If a person could get those benefits without the negative side effects, it would negate the argument.

One could counter that with the prohibition against drunkenness. Scripture is clear, being drunk is a sin. However, it never defines what drunk is. For one person a single glass of wine or beer gets them drunk. For another it may be several. The closest we can come to a universal standard would be what the government, the one put in place by God, defines as drunk.

So is it acceptable to place the drunkenness standard to cannabis? I would say it depends. If we are talking about the biblical prohibition on being drunk, where drunkenness causes us to say or do things contrary to Scripture, then it certainly does. If a person is using marijuana to escape their problems, then it is most certainly sin.

Of course, we must apply that prohibition properly—to Christians alone. We tend to forget the Bible is for believers to model their lives after, not non-believers. It is a misuse of the Word to force those who have not met the Savior to follow His lead.

A Christian needs to prayerfully consider this subject. It is neither fair nor appropriate to judge one person for holding a different view on this than you do. It is also inappropriate to force or trick other believers into taking the same view as you. There is some grace in this discussion, even if you are adamant about your position. How we handle this discussion can, and will, have a dramatic impact on the Kingdom and how the lost view God.

THE GOD-SHAPED HOLE

There is one aspect of this discussion we would be wrong to ignore. Many times mankind turns to substances like sex, alcohol, and marijuana in an attempt to fill the God-shaped hole in their hearts. God has wired all people to long for and desire Him. Throughout history, mankind has longed for a relationship with God. Even pagan cultures instinctively know there is something more to life. They worshiped anything and everything throughout history.

We live in a world that is increasingly hostile towards God. Scripture foretells this, but part of that is our own doing. The church is very unattractive to many because the people in the church are as broken as those outside. The lost expect us to be something we are not, when in reality, the only difference between believers and non-believers is our salvation. We are all broken and struggling through this life. The lost know this and the church often forgets it.

Regardless of what we are convicted of, there is always room for grace. Think for a moment about when you came to know Jesus as Savior. How much grace did God extend to you at that moment? For most of us, it would be impossible to quantify. With so much grace poured out on us, who are we to refuse to give it to another of God's creation.

Who knows? That grace may be the catalyst for someone to allow God to fill that hole they so desperately want filled. That is, after all, more important than being right.

9

LOVING THE MARGINALIZED

*We need to look marginalized people in our
community in the eye and listen to their stories
of struggle, heartache and impossibility.*

STEPHANIE LAND

*If the church does not identify with the marginalized, it
will itself be marginalized. This is God's poetic justice.*

TIMOTHY KELLER

I will be straight up with you, I might be a little biased in this chapter. The special needs community is my world and my mission. When I think of the marginalized in society, and the church, my mind immediately goes to families like mine. When we look at the subject of cannabis, the special needs community is often at the forefront of this discussion, at least in Colorado.

The marginalized are not limited to the family that may show up to church on a Sunday morning. Mental health issues encompass so many different groups. For those of us who live in large cities, we often see this manifested in homeless camps.

It is estimated that in 2020, there were over 120,000 homeless people in the United States with some form of severe mental illness.[1] So how does that fit into our discussion about cannabis? Approximately half of all individuals with a mental health illness experience some form of substance abuse, and that percentage increases in younger subjects.[2] That means approximately 60,000 homeless individuals with a severe mental illness also have a substance abuse problem.

A GROWING PROBLEM

The homeless epidemic in this country is growing by leaps and bounds. Part of this change is due to the economy, part due to the mental illness aspect, and part is due the change in cannabis laws. While it is not accurate to blame the homeless epidemic on recreational marijuana, there are certainly some who move to states like Colorado, without a job or housing, for that reason. Recreational users are not the only ones making that choice. It is not uncommon to see social media posts from desperate families who are considering moving to Colorado and living in a tent to get access to medical cannabis.

In a 2019 interview, a lieutenant for the El Paso County Colorado sheriff's department, the county where Colorado Springs is located, said,

> When recreational marijuana was legalized, we had about,
> on any given day about in El Paso County, 2 to 300 people

---

1. "Mentally Ill Homeless People in the U.S. by Sheltered Status 2020," Statista Research Department, March 24, 2021, https://www.statista.com/statistics/962300/number-mentally-ill-homeless -people-us-sheltered-status/.

2. "Part 1: The Connection between Substance Use Disorders and Mental Illness," National Institutes of Health, U.S. Department of Health and Human Services, April 13, 2021, https:// nida.nih.gov/publications/research-reports/common-comorbidities-substance-use-disorders/ part-1-connection-between-substance-use-disorders-mental-illness.

living on the streets that were homeless. Not taking advantage of shelter space. Today, a handful of years after, we have legalized marijuana, recreational marijuana, we have about 570 people that live on the street.[3]

The sheriff's department is seeing a quantifiable increase in the homeless population since the legalization of cannabis here in Colorado.

Does that mean cannabis reform is bad? Once again, the answer is maybe, but maybe not. A large portion of the homeless in Colorado Springs are coming from somewhere else. Those with drug abuse problems did not develop these issues the minute they crossed the state line. They simply moved to a state where they can get their fix without the fear of being arrested.

While this creates a burden for cities like Colorado Springs, it opens the door for greater access to this community. The advantage is the homeless are now concentrated, which makes it easier to diagnose, and treat, the mental health and substance abuse issues the homeless face. The problem is finding a way to care for this portion of the population in a safe and dignified way.

Many in this community do not realize they need help, while others simply do not want help. No one can force someone to accept help for a substance abuse problem or a mental health issue. This creates a complicated issue for both community leaders and law enforcement.

---

3. Yami Virgin, "Does Marijuana Legalization Contribute to Homelessness?" KABB, October 24, 2019, https://foxsanantonio.com/news/local/does-marijuana-legalization-contribute-to-homelessness.

THE CHURCH'S ROLE

So where does the church fit in? After all, this is a book for Christians.

Out of all the miracles Jesus performed, the majority were on those we could consider marginalized. He healed the lame, blind, sick, and leprose. He addressed the mental illness of those He came across. Instead of crossing to the other side of the road as the religious elite did in the parable of the good Samaritan, Jesus stepped up and loved on those society refused to.

It is the mission of the church to spread the gospel of Jesus Christ to the lost and dying world. This includes the homeless along with those who suffer from mental illness or substance abuse. These are the people who need the hope of Jesus Christ as much, if not more, than the social elite of our neighborhoods. If more of the church followed Christ's example, more Christians would be running to the homeless and disabled to introduce them to Jesus.

AN INCLUSIVE GOSPEL

The whole purpose of this book has been to educate the reader so that we can have grace-filled conversations about cannabis. If we only minister to those who think, look, and act like us, the conversation is easy. But that is not what we are called to do.

> The Spirit of the Lord is on me, because he has anointed me to preach good news to the poor. He has sent me to proclaim release to the captives and recovery of sight to the blind, to set free the oppressed, to proclaim the year of the Lord's favor. (Luke 4:18–19)

Jesus said his mission was to bring the good news to those who were suffering. He came to set all free from sin and death, but he had a special place for the marginalized in society, one he passed on to the church.

> Jesus came near and said to them, "All authority has been given to me in heaven and on earth. Go, therefore, and make disciples of **all** nations, baptizing them in the name of the Father and of the Son and of the Holy Spirit, teaching them to observe everything I have commanded you. (Matthew 28:18–20; emphasis mine)

Jesus said all nations—literally "people groups." That includes those who do not look like us or think like us. It includes those who's brains or bodies do not work like ours. The gospel is for all.

OF GRACE, NOT SALT

Relationships are not destroyed so much by our position on a subject but how we convey that position. If we are going to be a church that reaches the marginalized in society, we must be aware of how much salt is in our speech.

Are you willing to listen to an opposing view without trying to argue your point, even if the opposing view is not biblical?

Please don't misunderstand what I am saying. It would be wrong, no matter what, to walk into a homeless camp and condone drug abuse. It would also be wrong to support a special needs parent's desire to shun all traditional medications when their child is not responding to the current treatment. However, it is just as wrong to walk into this environment and let our conversations be used by Satan to drive people from Jesus.

> Act wisely toward outsiders, making the most of the time. Let your speech always be gracious, seasoned with salt, so that you may know how you should answer each person. (Colossians 4:5–6)

This is the hard work of making disciples. We have a fine line to walk between speaking truth and loving the lost. Too much truth all at once turns the lost away, while too little truth will never show them the true Christ. This is even more difficult when we attempt to reach those whom the church has more often than not ignored.

10

THE ART OF CREATING FRICTION

A gem cannot be polished without friction,
nor a man perfected without trials.

LUCIUS ANNAEUS SENECA

Friction, at times, can be a bad thing. If we have too much friction in an automotive engine, the engine stops working. A certain amount of friction in an engine is a good thing, but without the oil lubricating the parts, death of the engine is certain.

But friction is not always bad. There is such a thing as friction welding. One piece of material is rubbed rapidly against another. The friction produces heat, which in turn melts the two pieces of material. This permanently bonds the pieces into one.

Where friction seeks to bond things together, tension tries to pull objects apart. In the engineering world this is always a consideration. Sometimes introducing a little tension into a structure is what it needs to keep the building standing; other times it will bring it crumbling down.

So why did we go from cannabis to engineering?

TENSE CONVERSATIONS

The cannabis conversation is one that often ends up creating tension in the church world, especially if each side talks at, instead of to, the other. My heart for this book is not to tell you what to think or tell you what is right, but to encourage fruitful conversations. Subjects like cannabis are tense because we make them that way.

Think about the last time you had a hard conversation with a child, spouse, or friend that did not end well. Did you hear the other side? Did they hear you? Likely not. Nine times out of ten, when my wife and I fight over something, the reason we are arguing is because one of us does not feel heard by the other. When a person does not feel heard, most of the time the natural reaction is to get defensive. This usually causes the other person to get defensive, and things go bad.

This is where the tension comes in. Each person's view on the subject is pulling on their thoughts and beliefs, which drive the conversation. The problem is that these views pull the individuals in separate directions, most of the time away from the common ground. Left unchecked, that tension creates cracks in the body of Christ and can ultimately destroy the local church.

Tension always attempts to separate. That is not always bad thing, at least at first. Left unchecked, tension will build up and ultimately destroy relationships and the body of Christ. Our job is not to live in the tension, but to change the tension into friction.

IRON SHARPENS IRON

Solomon, the wisest man who ever lived, wrote, "Iron sharpens iron, and one person sharpens another" (Proverbs 27:17). This is a well-quoted verse of the Bible. Pastors use it to urge people to be in small groups or Bible studies. Christians fall back on it to explain to new believers why they need community. This one verse sums up why we need one another, and the local church.

Have you ever really thought about how iron sharpens iron?

To sharpen a piece of iron, it must be rubbed against another surface. The rubbing of the materials removes a small amount of the iron to create a sharp edge. The friction between the two pieces is what does the work of sharpening. Too much friction and the pieces, in theory, would stick together; too little friction will not produce a sharp edge.

Some people will say friction is a bad thing, but is it really? The more we rub against other Christian's beliefs, the sharper we each become. Put a little more pressure into the conversation and we begin to fuse together into one stronger, unified weapon against the forces of evil.

A THIN LINE

It sounds simple, right? Unfortunately it is not as easy as it sounds. Mankind, in its fallen state, struggles to get the right amount of pressure needed to create the sharpest edge possible. Much like getting a razor's edge on a knife, the conversations that lead to sharpness take practice and patience. Too little pressure will not produce results; too much produces a damaged edge.

I believe part of the struggle we have when it comes to sharpening one another is cultural. How many times have you heard that friction in the church is a bad thing? Paul wrote, "If possible, as far as it depends on you, live at peace with everyone" (Romans 12:18). Peace, especially in the church, should be sought, but not a friction-free congregation.

The church often confuses tension and friction. Some reading this will likely say they are the same thing. I would argue they are not; one is bad and one is good. The first, and hardest, step is to identify if it is tension or friction. Are the conversations happening in the church making stronger disciples, or are they creating division among the believers?

THE LITMUS TEST

Not sure if your conversations are creating tension or friction? Here are a few questions to ask yourself:

- Am I able to explain what the other person's view was to a third party?

- Did I learn something new from this conversation?

- Is my view of the other person the same or better than before?

- Do I look forward to seeing the other person again?

- Do I have a desire to learn more?

- Do I have more questions for the other party?

Now, go ask the other party the same questions.

If the answer to any of these questions is no, then the conversation is headed toward tension rather than friction. Realizing that tension can be caused by how a conversation goes is the first step towards creating the peace Paul called all believers to.

NOT BAD, NOT GOOD

Tension is a necessary evil, so to speak. In the engineering world it plays a vital role in building design. This is just as true in building God's Kingdom. Tension puts us on notice. It drives change and causes the Christian to seek God. Tension is a catalyst for growth, provided it is recognized for what it is. Resolving to live in the tension we create is not good or healthy. Tension must always be transitioned to friction if the church is to be healthy and effective for the Kingdom of God.

When it comes to the cannabis discussion, people need to be aware that it often starts in tension but cannot end there. The key to moving from unhealthy tension to healthy friction starts with knowledge. The more we know, the better we are. There is nothing wrong with admitting mistakes, even if the other person acts as if there is. Promoting peace often begins with the simple phrase, "I was wrong."

True peace within the body of Christ comes from healthy conversations and open hearts. We cannot bring peace by ignoring our personalities, differing opinions, and varying conversation styles. Peace will not be achieved if we forget that sin entered the world in the Garden of Eden, which leaves us living in a broken, imperfect world. Grace saved the Christian from an eternity apart from God. It is our responsibility to show grace to others when we have the delicate conversations.

As you begin, or continue, to have the cannabis conversation, be mindful that your opinion likely creates tension with the person you are talking to. Embrace that tension, but do not be content to live in it. It is important to do the hard work of moving from tension to friction. As hard as it is to hear, if the tension persists, the issue may be you. No one wants to hear that, but after all, the only person you are able to change is you.

TIPS TO MOVING FROM TENSION TO FRICTION

- Lead with prayer—days before your conversation.
- Ask the Spirit to bring an open heart that allows God to lead.
- Understand your personality and communication styles.
- Restate the other person's viewpoint in your own words.
- Ask for clarification if you do not understand.
- Listen more than you speak.
- Realize you might be wrong, and that's okay.
- Walk away if the time is not right or emotions are taking control.

Perhaps the most important thing is being willing to agree to disagree without thinking the other party is wrong. There are two sides to every argument, and unless Scripture is explicit, Christians must wrestle through this together. There are many things in this life which are not easy. Some of those we make more difficult than God ever intended for them to be. Allow the friction in this conversation to shapen and hone you to a razors edge.

EPILOGUE

The world is a thing of utter inordinate complexity and
richness and strangeness that is absolutely awesome.

DOUGLAS ADAMS

We have spent ten chapters on a subject that few would have ever thought we would be discussing in a church setting. I can also tell you, as I have done research and discussed this subject with those in the church, it has been an eye-opening ride. I have encountered those who are adamant that cannabis is a direct path to Satan and others who freely admit to recreational use.

I am thankful you have made it to the end of the book, especially if you started reading this reluctantly. I am not naïve. I know that by this point I have offended some. That is to be expected. The subject of cannabis is a touchy one in the church, and it likely always will be.

This is such a vital discussion to have if we are going to truly be the church in the twenty-first century. Cannabis is not going away, and is likely only the beginning, as we are seeing in Colorado. The city of Denver has approved the sale of psychedelic mushrooms and a measure is on the 2022 ballot to legalize mushrooms statewide. I fear, at this rate, it will only be a matter of time before the extreme liberals push for the legalizaion of drugs like heroin and LSD.

I am convinced this is an unfortunate side effect of cannabis legalization, at least in liberal states like Colorado, that we need to prepare for. There needs to be a balance between the medicinal, and even recreational, use of cannabis and curtailing the legalization of harder drugs. This is where the church must step up and lead.

However, to do so we must change the way we have the cannabis discussion. The time has come to open our minds, and more importantly our hearts, to have Christ-centered discussions about things that make us uncomfortable. The church must lead the country in a God-centered direction, but to do so we must be heard and taken seriously. That only happens when we hear, not just listen to, those who do not uphold the things of God, whether inside or outside the church.

The war may be won, but the church in the United States is losing the battle. The numbers of those who profess to be Christians is dropping every year. To many people, church is extremely unattractive. This is in part due to the inability to have civil conversations with the lost. The lost desperately want to be heard, not just preached at.

Theodore Roosevelt put it well: "No one cares how much you know, until they know how much you care." Are we, as the universal church, letting people know how much we care? Do we hear those who are hurting and try to understand, or do we simply recite Scripture as if they can understand it?

We seem to have forgotten in the church in this country that the Word of God is for believers. We cannot, and should not, attempt to hold the lost to the standard we should hold other Christians to. Introduce them to the Savior first, then let the Holy Spirit convict. Speak truth from the perspective of a messenger, not judge and jury.

We are called to create disciples of Christ. This involves teaching new Christians to think critically about things and prayerfully filter their thoughts through the lens of Scripture. Teach immature Christians to rely on God, not man, to provide the wisdom. When we do that, we create disciples who own their faith.

I hope you have gotten to this point and feel more educated on the topic of cannabis. Perhaps more important, I hope you can say that you own your personal conviction on the subject—to the point where you do not feel the need to argue it. Be open to discussions on the subject, and always be looking for the Spirit to move.

May God bless you and use this book to see lives changed in your community.

www.ingramcontent.com/pod-product-compliance
Lightning Source LLC
Chambersburg PA
CBHW030510130626
46549CB00007B/2918